Top 30 Most

Burrito Recipes

A Burrito Cookbook
with Beef, Lamb, Pork, Chorizo, Chicken and Turkey

by Graham Bourdain

Thank you for getting
Top 30 Most Delicious Burrito Recipes.

We hope you find the recipes as tasteful and delicious as we do.

If you want to get all the other recipe books by Graham Bourdain then:

Check out and follow the Author Page on Amazon
(See Kindle Version for direct link)

Enjoy the recipes and happy cooking
sincerely, Graham Bourdain

Disclaimer

Reasonable care has been taken to ensure that the information presented in this book is accurate. However, the reader should understand that the information provided does not constitute legal, medical or professional advice of any kind.

No Liability: this product is supplied "as is" and without warranties. All warranties, express or implied, are hereby disclaimed. Use of this product constitutes acceptance of the "No Liability" policy. If you do not agree with this policy, you are not permitted to use or distribute this product.

We shall not be liable for any losses or damages whatsoever

(including, without limitation, consequential loss or damage) directly or indirectly arising from the use of this product.

Table of Contents

Beef Burritos

Ground Beef Burritos..8

Spicy Beef Burritos 10

Beef and Bean Burritos...12

Sloppy Beef Burritos...14

Skirt Steak Burritos...16

Lamb Burritos

Braised Lamb Burritos 18

Roast Lamb Burritos 20

Slow-roasted Cajun Lamb Burritos....................................22

Curry Lamb Burritos 24

Cumin-Ancho Lamb Burritos..26

Pork Burritos

Poselequeso Burritos...28

Slow Cooker Chile Verde Pork Burritos 30

Chipotle Pork Burritos 32

Smothered Sweet Pork Burritos 34

Pork, Rice and Bean Burritos 36

Chorizo Burritos

Chorizo, Potato and Queso Burritos.......................................38

Cauliflower-Chorizo Burritos 40

Chorizo, Potato and Egg Burritos 42

Chorizo, Potato Burritos 44

Chorizo Salsa Burritos..46

Chicken Burritos

Chipotle Chicken Burritos 48

Shredded Mexican Chicken Burritos 50

Mojo Chicken Burritos..52

Tequila-Orange BBQ Chicken Burritos...................................54

Chicken and Bean Burritos..56

Turkey Burritos

Turkey Chili Burritos..58

Turkey Burritos with Salsa and Cilantro 60

Teriyaki Turkey Burritos 62

Turkey and Black Bean Burritos 64

Cajun Rice and BBQ Turkey Burritos 66

Ground Beef Burritos

Prep: 20 min. Cook: 15 min. Ready in: 35 min. Servings: 4

Ingredients:

Meat filling:

1 pound ground beef

1 ½ oz. dry burrito or taco mix

1 cup water

Salsa:

1 ½ medium roma tomatoes

½ garlic clove, peeled

1 green onion

1 ½ oz. chopped chilies

½-1 whole fresh jalapeno

1/8 cup cilantro

½ tsp. Mexican chili powder

½ tbsp. lime juice

to taste salt and pepper

Tortilla and condiments:

4 burrito-size tortillas

6 tbsp. sour cream

1 cup four-cheese Mexican blend cheese

2 roma tomatoes, diced

4 green onions, sliced into rings

Cooking Directions:

Start by making the salsa. Char the tomatoes over the flame of a hot broiler or similar. Turn them until the peel blisters. Slip off the peel, and the flesh should still be firm. Remove the green stem core and the tomatoes in half. Use a spoon to discard the seeds and discard. In the food processor, drop in the garlic, cilantro, green onions and jalapenos into the bowl of the food processor to chop for just a few seconds. Add the tomatoes, Serrano chili, the chopped green chilies, chili powder and lime juice. Process until the texture is between a relish and a puree. Add salt and pepper to taste.

Place the salsa in the fridge until ready for use.

Next take a large pot and add 1 cup of water and the burrito seasoning mix. Add the ground beef in the liquid and break it down, so there are no chunks. Bring the mix to a boil, then reduce the heat and let it simmer. Stir occasionally, until the liquid has been absorbed.

Put each tortilla on a plate and microwave it on high for 15 seconds. Remove the tortilla from the microwave and spread 2 tbsp. of sour cream, slight off center, on the tortilla. Place ¼ of the ground beef on top, then ¼ cup of the cheese blend and finish with 2 tbsp. of the salsa. Sprinkle on tomatoes and green onions.

Fold the front of the tortilla over the filling. Tuck the left and right sides of the tortilla inside as you roll and continue rolling until the tortilla is on its belly with the weight of the filling holding it together.

Enjoy

Spicy Beef Burritos

Prep: 30 min. Cook: 20 min. Ready in: 50 min. Servings: 6

Ingredients:

6 oz. jalapeno pepper, sliced

1 tomato, diced

1 (4 oz.) can chopped green chile peppers

1 green bell pepper, diced

1 onion, diced

1 ½ tbsp. hot sauce

¼ tsp. ground cayenne pepper

1 pound ground beef

1 (1 oz.) package burrito seasoning

1 (14 oz.) can refried beans

6 tortillas

1 (10 oz.) bag shredded lettuce

1 (8 oz.) container sour cream

1 (8oz.) pack shredded cheddar cheese

Cooking Directions:

Start by preheating a skillet over medium-high heat.

Take a large bowl and mix together jalapeno peppers, tomato, green chili peppers, green bell pepper, red bell pepper, onion, hot sauce and cayenne pepper.

Cook the beef in the preheated skillet, stirring to break up clumps, approx. 5 min. Drain excess grease. Add the jalapeno pepper mix and burrito seasoning. Cook until the flavors combine, approx. 10 min.

Pour refried beans into a saucepan over medium-low heat. Cook and stir until heated through, approx. 5 min.

Warm each tortilla in the microwave until soft, approx. 15 seconds. Spread a layer of refried beans on top. Divide the beef mix among the tortillas. Top with lettuce, sour cream and cheddar cheese.

Fold in the opposing edges of each tortillas and roll up into a burrito.

Enjoy

Beef and Bean Burritos

Prep: 15 min. Cook: 20 min. Ready in: 35 min. Servings: 4

Ingredients:

½ medium onion, diced,

1 pound ground beef

¼ tsp. ground cumin

¼ tsp. chili powder

¼ tsp. ground oregano

¼ tsp. salt

2 (7 oz.) cans Mexican tomato sauce / enchilada sauce

1 (14 oz.) can refried beans

¾ cup grated cheddar, extra for sprinkling

6 tortillas

½ cup fresh cilantro leaves

Cooking Directions:

Start by preheating the oven to 170-180 degrees F (80 degrees C). Place a skillet over medium heat and cook the onions until softened. Then add the ground beef and cook until the beef is cooked through. Add the cumin, chili powder, oregano and salt and stir to combine. Pour 2 cans of the Mexican tomato sauce into the meat let it simmer over low heat for 5 minutes.

Meanwhile, heat the refried beans in a saucepan over medium-low heat. Add the cheese, and stir it in till its melted. Remove from the heat. Heat the tortillas in the microwave for 1 minute, and then spread a small amount of beans on each tortilla. Add a small amount of the meat. Fold over the ends of the tortilla, and then roll them up. Repeat with the rest of the tortillas. Then place them in a large baking dish, cover with foil and keep warm in the oven.

When ready to serve, drizzle the remaining can of tomato sauce over all of the burritos and sprinkle with grated cheddar. Return to the oven for a couple of minutes to melt the cheese.

Sprinkle the burritos with cilantro leaves and serve.

Enjoy

Sloppy Beef Burritos

Prep: 30 min. Cook: 30 min. Ready in: 1 h Servings: 4

Ingredients:

1 pound ground beef

½ cup chopped onion

2 cloves garlic, minced

1 (14.5 oz.) can diced tomatoes with juice, divided

1 tbsp. Worcestershire sauce

1 ½ tsp. chili powder

1 tsp. paprika

1 tsp. dried oregano

¾ tsp. ground cumin

½ tsp. ground black pepper

2 cups refried beans

¼ tsp. ground cumin

1 (18 oz.) jar beef gravy

1 (10 oz.) can enchilada sauce

4 tortillas

2 cups shredded cheddar cheese, divided

1 cup sour cream, divided

¼ cup chopped onion, divided

¼ cup chopped tomatoes, divided

1 cup chopped lettuce, divided

Cooking Directions:

Start by preheating the oven to 375 degrees F (190 degrees C).

Place a skillet over medium heat. Cook and stir ground beef, 1/2 cup chopped onion, and garlic in the hot skillet until beef is browned and crumbly, approx. 8 min. Mix in half the can of diced tomatoes, Worcestershire sauce, chili powder, paprika, oregano, 3/4 tsp. cumin, and black pepper. Bring meat mixture to a boil over medium-high heat and cook for 5 minutes, stirring often.

Heat refried beans and 1/4 tsp. cumin in a saucepan over medium-low heat. Keep beans warm. Mix remaining half of diced tomatoes, beef gravy, and enchilada sauce in a separate saucepan; bring to a boil.

Microwave tortillas until they are soft and warm, approx. 30 seconds. Take a warmed tortilla and spoon ¼ of the beef mixture in a line down the center of the tortilla. Layer ¼ of the bean mixture on top of beef layer and spread 1/4 cup of cheddar cheese over the bean layer. Fold right and left edges of the tortilla over the ends of the filling and roll up tortilla to make a burrito. Place burrito seam side down into a baking dish. Repeat with remaining tortillas to make 4 burritos.

Pour gravy sauce over the burritos in the baking dish; top with remaining 1 cup cheddar cheese.

Bake burritos in the preheated oven until the cheese has melted, 15 to 20 minutes.

Place each burrito on a serving plate and spoon sauce from the baking dish over the burritos. Top each burrito with ¼ cup sour cream, 1 tsp. chopped onion and chopped tomato, and ¼ cup of chopped lettuce.

Enjoy

Skirt Steak Burritos

Prep: 30 min. Cook: 10 min. Ready in: 1 h 40 min. Servings: 6

Ingredients:

Marinade:

1 tbsp. black peppercorns

1 tbsp. whole white peppercorns

2 tbsp. whole coriander seeds

1 tbsp. red pepper flakes

2 tbsp. dark brown sugar

1 skirt steak, approx. 2 pounds, cut into 4 pieces

Onions:

6 cipolini or pearl onions, peeled and cut ¼ inch thick

2-3 tbsp. red wine vinegar

1 pinch granulated sugar

1 cup stemmed, washed and halved cherry tomatoes

Olive oil

3 limes, ½ lime juice, remaining limes cut into wedges

Kosher salt

½ washed and dried cilantro leaves

16 oz. cheddar, grated

6 tortillas

Cooking Directions:

Start by adding the black peppercorns, white peppercorns, coriander seeds, and pepper flakes to a pan over medium heat. Toast them until they start to smell aromatic, approx. 1-2 min. Crush them in a mortar and pestle. Add the sugar and salt and toss to combine.

Coat both sides of each steak with a layer of the peppercorn mixture. Put the steaks on a baking sheet, cover with plastic wrap and refrigerate for 1 hour or overnight.

Put the onion slices in a bowl and gently pull them apart until you have a lot of individual rounds. Add the red wine vinegar and sugar. Coat the onions with the vinegar. Press them down into the bowl and cover with plastic wrap. Set aside to marinate until ready to serve.

Heat 2 skillets large enough to hold the steaks. Add 2 tbsp. of the oil to each pan. When the oil begins to smoke lightly, season the steak with salt and gently put the steaks in the hot oil. Cook at high heat, approx. 2-3 min., on each side. If the steak becomes too brown, lower the heat slightly as it cooks. Remove the steak and allow it to "rest" for 10 min. Wipe off and use the skillets or a microwave to warm the tortillas.

Take a bowl and combine the cherry tomatoes with the juice of ½ lime, salt to taste, and the picked cilantro leaves. Mix and taste for seasoning.

Slice the steak into thin slices. Take a tortilla and arrange some of the meat, the tomato mixture, cheese and pickled onions in a line in the center of the tortilla. Fold the edges into the center and roll it up into a burrito. Keep it warm in the oven while you roll the others.

When finished remove the burritos from the oven and serve warm.

Enjoy

Braised Lamb Burritos

Prep: 30 min. Cook: 15 min. Ready in: 45 min. Servings: 6

Ingredients:

For the lamb:

4 boneless leg of lamb

1 tbsp. vegetable oil

Kosher salt and black pepper

1 ½ cups dry white wine or water

1 tbsp. ground cumin

4 medium cloves garlic, peeled and smashed

1 large carrot, cut into 1-inch thick rounds

1 onion, peeled and cut into 8 wedges

2 tbsp. pomegranate molasses

1 ½ tsp. fresh lemon juice

2 tbsp. unsalted butter

6 tortillas

For the tahini sauce:

2 cloves garlic, minced

2 tbsp. fresh lemon juice

½ cup whole-milk Greek Yoghurt

½ cup tahini

3 tbsp. extra-virgin olive oil

For the pickled cabbage:

1 ½ tsp. extra-virgin olive oil

2 cups thinly sliced red cabbage

½ tsp. pomegranate molasses

1 tbsp. sherry vinegar

¼ tsp. granulated sugar

Kosher salt and ground black pepper

Cooking Directions:

Start by adding pepper, coriander and cumin seeds to a dry pan and toast them until they start to crackle. Pour them straight into a coffee grinder and blend the seeds to a fine powder.

Then take a mixing bowl and add all the spices, garlic and salt to the lamb and mix it well. Form the mix into 6 evenly sized patties. Moving on to the sauce. After weighing, open up the dried peppers to shake out the seeds. Put the peppers in a saucepan with the water and boil over medium heat until ¼ cup of liquid remains. Add the peppers, cooking liquid, sour cream, oil, garlic and lime to the blender, and blend it until smooth. Add salt and cream and blend again until the mix gets a saucy consistency.

Cook the lamb patties on a frying pan for approx. 4-5 min. per side for medium rare. Put about 1 tsp. of sauce on each side of the hamburger bun and crumble Cojita cheese on top. Assemble the burger with tomato slices, onion and lettuce and serve.

Enjoy

Roast Lamb Burritos

Prep: 25 min. Cook: 45 min. Ready in: 1 h 10 min. Servings: 2

Ingredients:

1 pound roast beef

½ tsp. kosher salt

½ tsp. garlic powder

¼ tsp. ground black pepper

1 tbsp. vegetable oil

1 onion, chopped

1 clove garlic, minced

4 tomatoes, chopped

2 cups chopped cooked roast beef

1 (8 oz.) jar prepared taco sauce

1 (4 oz.) can diced green chili peppers

½ tsp. cumin

1/8 tsp. red pepper flakes

1 ½ cups shredded cheddar cheese

2 cups shredded lettuce

4 tortillas

Cooking Directions:

Start by preheating the oven to 375 degrees F (190 degrees C). If the roast is untied, tie at 3 inch intervals with cotton twine. Place the roast in a pan, and season with salt, garlic powder, and pepper. Roast in the oven for 20 min. (20 min. per pound.) Remove from the oven, and let rest for 15-20 min. Then slice it in thin slices.

Next, start heating a skillet over medium-high heat. Drizzle it with the oil. Stir in the onion and garlic, and cook until tender and transparent, approx. 5 min. Mix in the tomatoes, roast beef, taco sauce, chili peppers, cumin, and red pepper flakes. Bring the mixture to a boil. Reduce heat to medium, and let simmer for approx. 25 min. or until thickened.

Warm the tortillas in the oven or microwave. Spread about 2/3 cup of the lamb mixture in the center of each tortilla. Sprinkle evenly with cheese and lettuce. Fold over the sides and ends to roll each tortilla up into a burrito. Serve warm.

Enjoy

Slow-roasted Cajun Lamb Burritos

Prep: 10 min. Cook: 3 h 35 min. Ready in: 3 h 45 min. Servings: 4

Ingredients:

4 pounds Lamb Shoulder Roast Bone In

¼ cup olive oil

1 tbsp. Cajun seasoning

1 lemon, zested

2 garlic cloves, crushed

½ tsp. salt flakes

1 cup chicken stock

2 cups microwave brown rice

2 stick celery, finely chopped

3 spring onions, thinly sliced

1 tsp. Cajun seasoning

¼ cup chopped coriander

1 tbsp. lemon juice

8 tortillas

½ cup roasted capsicum

Coriander leaves, to serve

Greek-style yoghurt, to serve

Cooking Directions:

Start by preheating the oven to 300 degrees F (150 degrees C). Place a rack in a large roasting tray. Use a small, sharp knife to make shallow cuts on the surface of lamb. Season. Heat 2 tsp. oil in a large frying pan over high heat. Add the lamb and cook, turning, for 5 min. or until browned all over. Remove from heat.

Combine Cajun seasoning, lemon zest, 1 garlic clove, salt and 2 tbsp. oil in a medium bowl. Add the lamb and turn to coat. Place lamb on rack in the roasting tray. Pour stock into the tray. Cover with foil and roast for 3 – 3 ½ hours or until the lamb is browned and very tender. Remove the foil and shred meat with a fork.

Meanwhile, heat the rice following the packet instructions. Heat the remaining oil in a medium saucepan over medium heat. Add the celery and cook, stirring, for 5 min. Add the remaining garlic, spring onion and extra Cajun seasoning and cook, stirring, for 2 min or until fragrant. Add rice, chopped coriander and lemon juice and stir to combine. Season.

Assemble the burritos by dividing the rice mixture among the tortillas. Top with lamb, capsicum, coriander leaves and a dollop of yoghurt. Fold in sides and ends rolling up into a burrito. Serve warm.

Enjoy

Curry Lamb Burritos

Prep: 1 h. Cook: 15 min. Ready in: 1 h 15 min. Servings: 4

Ingredients:

1 pound ground lamb

½ white onion, diced

1 serrano pepper, diced

3 cloves garlic, minced

1 tsp. ginger, minced

1 tbsp. curry powder

½ tbsp. garam masala

¼ tsp salt

¼ tsp black pepper

1 /4 cup water

4 tortillas

2 cups tomatoes, diced

Sauce:

1.5 cup yoghurt

juice from 1 lemon

¼ tsp. salt

1 tbsp. dried dill

2 cloves minced garlic

Cooking Directions:

Start by making the sauce. Take a bowl and mix the yoghurt, juice from 1 lemon, salt, dried dill and garlic. Cover and refrigerate for 1 hour or overnight.

Next, take a frying pan or stock pot. Cook the ground lamb over medium heat until cooked through. Strain off fat and set lamb aside.

In the same pan, cook the onions and serrano over medium heat until the onions are translucent. Add the garlic and ginger and cook 1 more minute. Add curry powder, garam masala, salt and pepper, stir and cook for one more minute. Add ¼ cup of water and stir again.

Add the lamb back to the pan, stir and reduce until most liquid has been absorbed or evaporated.

Assemble the burritos by placing ¼ of meat on a warm tortilla, add ¼ of tomatoes and yoghurt sauce. Fold up and serve.

Enjoy

Cumin-Ancho Lamb Burritos

Prep: 25 min. Cook: 6 min. Ready in: 31 min. Servings: 4

Ingredients:

1 tbsp. vegetable oil

¾ pound ground lamb

1 ½ tsp. ground cumin

1 ½ tsp. unsweetened cocoa powder

1 ½ tsp. ancho chili powder

¼ tsp. crushed red pepper

½ small red onion, finely chopped

Salt and ground pepper

1 cup canned refried beans

4 tortillas

2 cups (6 oz.) grated cheese

1 medium tomato, chopped

1 cup cilantro leaves

½ cup jarred salsa

1 cup sour cream

Cooking Directions:

Start by preheating the oven to 450 degrees F (230 degrees C). Heat the vegetable oil in a large skillet. Add the ground lamb, cumin, cocoa powder, chili powder and crushed red pepper. Cook over moderate heat, stirring to break up the ground lamb, until the meat is cooked through, approx. 6 min. Stir in the onion, season with salt and pepper and transfer the lamb to a bowl. Add the refried beans to the skillet and cook until they are hot.

Take the tortillas and spoon ¼ of the ground lamb across the center of each tortilla. Top each with ¼ of the refried beans, cheese, chopped tomato, cilantro and salsa and roll up the tortillas to burritos, folding in the sides and top.

Put the burritos in a large baking dish and bake them for approx. 10 min. or until hot. Serve the burritos with the sour cream.

Enjoy

Poselequeso Burritos

Prep: 15 min. Cook: 10 min. Ready in: 25 min. Servings: 8

Ingredients:

1 pound shredded cooked pork

4 cups drained canned white hominy

1/8 bunch fresh cilantro, chopped

1 tsp. dried oregano

1 tsp. minced garlic

1 tsp. chili paste

¼ tsp. ground cumin

¼ tsp. lemon pepper

8 tortillas

½ (16 oz.) package shredded cheddar cheese

Cooking Directions:

Start by taking a large skillet and heat it over medium heat. Add the pork, hominy, cilantro, oregano, garlic, chili paste, cumin and lemon pepper. Cook and stir until heated through, approx. 10-15 min.

Put the tortillas on a plate and microwave in the microwave for 10 seconds or heat in the oven.

Spoon the pork mixture into each tortillas and top with cheddar cheese.

Fold the sides over the filling and roll up the tortillas into burritos. Serve warm.

Enjoy

Slow Cooker Chile Verde Pork Burritos

Prep: 10 min. Cook: 6 h 30 min. Ready in: 6 h 40 min. Servings: 6

Ingredients:

1 pound stew pork meat

1 (15 oz.) bottle green taco sauce

½ medium onion, diced

1 chicken bullions cube

2 garlic cloves, minced

1 (4 oz.) can green chilies

¼ tsp. pepper

¾ tbsp. cumin

¼ cayenne

1 can refried beans

6 tortillas

1 ½ cups shredded Mexican cheese blend

Cooking Directions:

Start by spraying the slow cooker with cooking spray.

Add the pork, green sauce, onion, bouillon, garlic, green chilies, pepper, cumin and cayenne to the slow cooker and cook for 6 hours.

After the pork has cooked, lay out the tortillas and place a medium spoon full of beans in the middle of the tortillas. Spoon a few chunks of pork onto the top of the beans and sprinkle some cheese over the meat.

Fold up the sides of the tortillas and roll them into burritos. Place the burritos in a baking dish sprayed with cooking spray.

Fill the baking dish with burritos and pour the chili verde sauce, meat and all, over the burritos. Sprinkle cheese over the top and bake for approx. 30 min. at 350 degrees F (180 degrees C) until the cheese is melted.

Serve warm with sour cream.

Enjoy

Chipotle Pork Burritos

Prep: 10 min. Cook: 25 min. Ready in: 35 min. Servings: 4

Ingredients:

2 tbsp. vegetable oil

12 oz. ground lean pork

1 onion, finely diced

2 garlic cloves, minced

1 tsp. ground cumin

1 tsp. ground coriander

¼ tsp. salt

¼ tsp. pepper

1 cup mild salsa

2 chipotle peppers, minced

¼ cup fresh coriander

4 tortillas

1 cup cheddar cheese, shredded

1 small sweet green pepper, diced

½ tomato, diced

Cooking Directions:

Start by taking a large skillet and heat it over medium heat. Pour in half of the oil and add the pork. Fry and break up the pork, until no longer pink, approx. 8 min. Remove the pork from the skillet, set it aside and drain the fat from the skillet.

In the same skillet, heat the remaining oil. Fry the onion, garlic, cumin, ground coriander, salt and pepper, stirring occasionally, until the onion is softened, approx. 5 min.

Return the pork to the pan. Add salsa and chipotle pepper. Let the mix simmer, stirring until thickened and saucy, approx. 5 min. Stir in fresh coriander.

Spoon ¼ of the pork mixture onto the center of each tortilla. Sprinkle evenly with cheese, green pepper and tomato.

Fold bottom edge over the filling, then the sides and roll up into a burrito.

Place the tortillas on a rimmed baking sheet and bake them in the oven at 400 degrees F (200 degrees C) for approx. 7 min. Turn once. Serve warm.

Enjoy

Smothered Sweet Pork Burritos

Prep: 20 min. Cook: 4 h 30 min. Ready in: 4 h 50 min. Servings: 6

Ingredients:

For the burritos:

2 ½ pounds pork roast

Salt and pepper

1 tbsp. oil

1-2 tsp. liquid smoke

½ cup water

½ cup packed light or dark brown sugar

2 (15 oz. each) cans green enchilada sauce

½ tsp. chili powder

1 tsp. salt

½ tsp. pepper

1 (15 oz.) can black beans, rinsed and drained

½ cup chopped cilantro

8 oz. cheddar cheese, grated

6 tortillas

For the cilantro lime rice:

½ tbsp. butter

1 cup long-grain white rice

2 cups low-sodium chicken broth

¾ tsp. salt

¼ tsp. freshly ground black pepper

juice and zest of 1 lime

2 tbsp. chopped cilantro

¼ tsp. cumin

Cooking Directions:

Start by taking a large skillet and heat the oil over medium-high heat. Cut the pork into 2-3 large pieces. Season each piece with salt and pepper. Add the pieces of pork to the skillet and brown them on each side, approx. 2-3 min total. Transfer the pork to the insert of a slow cooker.

Add the liquid smoke and ½ cup water. Cook on high for 4 ½ hours or on low for 8 hours.

While the pork is cooking, prepare the rice. Take a skillet, melt the butter and add the rice. Stir, letting the rice and butter cook for 1-2 min. Add the broth, salt, pepper lime juice and zest, cilantro and cumin and bring to a boil.

Reduce heat, cover and cook for 15-16 min. Remove from heat and let stand, covered, for 10 min. The rice can be made ahead and refrigerated until ready to assemble the burritos.

Remove the pork from the slow cooker and shred into bite-sized pieces. Take a large bowl and mix the shredded pork with the brown sugar, ½ cup of the green sauce, chili powder, salt and pepper. Stir in the beans, rice and cilantro to the pork mixture.

Lightly grease a baking dish with cooking spray and spread about ½ cup of the green sauce on the bottom.

Warm the tortillas lightly in a skillet or in the microwave. Scoop about ½ cup of the pork mixture into each tortillas and sprinkle with a of cheese. Fold in the sides of the tortillas and roll up into burritos. Place the burritos seam-side down in the prepared baking dish. Pour the remaining sauce over the burritos and sprinkle with remaining cheese. Bake at 350 degrees F (180 degrees C) for approx. 15-20min until heated through and top is slightly golden.

Serve warm.

Enjoy

Pork, Rice and Bean Burritos

Prep: 25 min. Cook: 6 h Ready in: 6 h 25 min. Servings: 4

Ingredients:

For the spice rub:

1 ¼ tsp. garlic powder

1 tsp. onion powder

¾ tsp. salt

½ tsp. white pepper

½ tsp. pepper

¼ tsp ground cumin

¼ tsp dried oregano

¼ tsp. cayenne pepper

For the burritos:

2 pounds shoulder roast

½ cup water

1 tbsp. beef bouillon granules

4 tortillas

1 ½ cups canned pinto beans, rinsed and drained

1 ½ cups cooked Spanish rice

Cooking Directions:

Start by taking a small bowl and mix the garlic powder, onion powder, salt, white pepper, pepper, ground cumin, dried oregano and cayenne pepper. Rub the mix over the pork and transfer the pork to a slow cooker.

In a small bowl, mix water and beef granules. Pour the mix around the roast. Cook, covered, on low 6-8 hours or until the meat is tender.

Remove the roast from the slow cooker and let it cool slightly.

Reserve ½ cup cooking juices and discard the remaining juices.

Shred the pork with forks and return the pork and reserved juices to the slow cooker. Heat through.

Spoon 1/3 cup shredded pork across the center of each tortilla. Top with 1/3 cup of beans and rice.

Fold over the sides and roll up into burritos.

Serve with condiments of your desire.

Enjoy

Chorizo, Potato and Queso Burritos

Prep: 13 min. Cook: 22 min. Ready in: 45 min. Servings: 6

Ingredients:

For the queso:

1 pound white American cheese, shredded

½ cup light cream

½ - 1 tbsp. oil

1 jalapeño, seeds removed, diced

¼ small purple onion, diced

1 roma tomato, diced

1 tbsp. chopped fresh cilantro

Black pepper to taste

For the chorizo mix:

12 oz. fresh Mexican chorizo, casings removed

1 green poblano pepper, diced

1 small yellow onion, diced

1 tbsp. fresh cilantro, diced

6-8 small red potatoes

1 tbsp. oil

¼ tsp. salt

¼ tsp. black pepper

6 tortillas

Cooking Directions:

Start by taking a large skillet and heating it over medium heat. Add the oil and sauté the jalapeño and onion until the pepper is tender and the onion is translucent.

Reduce the heat to medium low and in all of the shredded white American cheese and stir constantly.

When the cheese is nearly melted, begin stirring in half and half. Use more or less to get the consistency that you're looking for.

Add in the diced tomato, chopped cilantro and black pepper. Stir until everything is incorporated and the queso is smooth and creamy. Set it aside and start the chorizo mix.

Rinse the potatoes and pierce them with a fork. Microwave them for approx. 5 min. to get the cooking process going. Once the potatoes are partially cooked, cut them into small cubes.

Take a skillet and begin browning the chorizo and breaking it up. After cooking the chorizo a few minutes, add in the diced poblano pepper, and diced onion. Continue cooking until the chorizo is cooked through and the peppers and onions are tender.

Warm the tortillas in the microwave or heat on the skillet.

Take the tortillas and fill each one with ¾ cup of the chorizo/potato mix. Top with warm queso. Fold in the sides of the tortillas and roll up into burritos.

Serve warm.

Enjoy

Cauliflower-Chorizo Burritos

Prep: 10 min. Cook: 20 min. Ready in: 30 min. Servings: 8

Ingredients:

For the beans:

3 oz. raw pork chorizo, casings removed

½ small white onion, finely chopped

1 (15 oz.) can refried pinto beans

For the burritos:

2 tbsp. extra-virgin olive oil

1 small white onion, finely chopped

1 head cauliflower, florets finely chopped

Kosher salt and ground pepper

1 tbsp. chopped fresh oregano

8 tortillas

1 cup shredded Monterey Jack cheese

Cooking Directions:

Start by heating a medium saute pan over medium heat. Add the chorizo and cook, breaking up the meat, until golden, approx. 6 min. Remove the chorizo to paper towel and let it drain. Add the onion to the pan with the chorizo fat. Sauté until the onion is translucent, approx. 4 min. Return the chorizo to the pan. Add the refried beans to the mixture. Continue cooking for 5min and turn off the heat. Cover and keep warm.

Next, take a large sauté pan and heat the olive oil over medium-high heat. Add the onion and cook until translucent, approx. 3 min. Add the cauliflower and sauté until tender, approx. 5 min. Season with salt and pepper. Add the oregano. Turn off the heat and set aside.

Warm the tortillas in the microwave or heat them in a skillet.

Fill each tortilla with ¼ cup warm beans in the center, spreading it outwards to the sides. Add 2-3 tbsp. of the cauliflower mixture and 2 tbsp. of cheese. Fold in the sides and roll it up into a burrito.

Serve warm.

Enjoy

Chorizo, Potato and Egg Burritos

Prep: 15 min. Cook: 45 min. Ready in: 1 h Servings: 4

Ingredients:

1 large baking potato, peeled, and cut into ½ inch cubes

1 tsp. vegetable oil

12 oz. Mexican chorizo, casings removed

4 scallions, white parts discarded, green parts chopped

6 large eggs

1 tsp. olive oil

4 tortillas

2/3 cup Mexican melting cheese

½ cup fresh cilantro, chopped

½ cup salsa

1 avocado, halved, pitted, peeled, sliced

Cooking Directions:

Start by putting the chopped potato into a bowl along with 1 tsp. oil and a pinch of salt. Cover with plastic wrap. Place in microwave and cook on high for 4 min. Carefully remove plastic wrap. Potatoes should be tender. If not, recover and cook for another minute. Dump the potato cubes into a skillet set over medium heat. Cook, stirring occasionally, until potatoes are golden brown and slightly crisp. Set aside.

Meanwhile, add chorizo to a large skillet set over medium-high heat. Cook, breaking it up with a wooden spoon, until cooked through, approx. 5 min. Add the scallions, stir well, and cook for another 30 sec. Transfer chorizo to a bowl and set aside.

Clean the skillet, and then pour in the olive oil and set back over medium heat. Whisk together the eggs in a medium-sized bowl. Season with salt and pepper. Add the eggs to skillet and cook, stirring with a wooden spoon, until softly scrambled. Immediately transfer eggs to a second bowl and set aside.

Clean skillet again, and then warm over medium heat. Warm the tortillas in the skillet or in the microwave.

Place ¼ of the potatoes, chorizo, eggs, cheese, cilantro, salsa and avocado on each of the four warmed tortillas. Fold the sides of the tortillas over the filling and then roll them up into a burrito.

Serve warm.

Enjoy

Chorizo, Potato Burritos

Prep: 20 min. Cook: 8 min. Ready in: 20 min. Servings: 6

Ingredients:

14 oz. chorizo, casings removed, finely chopped

1 cup of refried beans

½ cup of grated cheese

6 tortillas

2 avocados, halved, pitted, peeled, sliced

2 tomatoes, diced

¼ of a lettuce heat, chopped

½ onion, chopped

½ cup of Mexican Cream

1 tbsp. of olive oil

½ tbsp.

Cooking Directions:

Start by taking a skillet and heating it over medium-high heat. Add 1 tbsp. of olive oil. Add the onion dices and cook them until transparent, approx. 1 min, stir regularly.

Toss in the chopped chorizo and cook it for approx. 4 min, until it is well cooked, stir regularly. Then set aside.

Heat 1 cup of refried beans in the microwave for approx. 1 ½ min, until they are well heated, then reserve.

Then heat the tortillas in the microwave.

Assemble the burritos by taking the tortillas and spoon some of the refried beans in the center of each tortillas. Add the grated cheese, chorizo, tomato dices, avocado slices, lettuce strips, Mexican cream and a pinch of salt.

Fold the sides of the tortillas over the filing and roll them up into burritos.

Serve warm.

Enjoy

Chorizo Salsa Burritos

Prep: 15 min. Cook: 20 min. Ready in: 35 min. Servings: 4

Ingredients:

1 small potato, peeled and cut into ½ inch cubes

Kosher salt

9 tsp. olive oil

1 pound Mexican chorizo, casings removed

4 tortillas

8 large eggs

Ground black pepper

1 cup shredded cheddar cheese

½ cup chopped cilantro

½ cup roasted tomato salsa

Cooking Directions:

Start by heating the oven to 300 degrees F (150 degrees C). Take a microwave-safe bowl and toss together cubed potato, a pinch of salt, and 3 tsp. of the olive oil. Cover the bowl with plastic wrap and microwave for 4 min., stirring halfway through. Check to see if the potatoes are tender. If not, continue to microwave in 30 second bursts until done.

Warm 3 tsp. of the olive oil in a large frying pan over medium-high heat. Add the potatoes and cook until browned, approx. 5 min. Transfer to a medium bowl and set aside. Crumble the chorizo into the same pan and cook, stirring and breaking up the meat, until cooked through, approx. 5 min.

Add the chorizo to the bowl with the potatoes and cover to keep warm. Wipe off the frying pan.

Put the tortillas in the oven to warm while you cook the eggs. Whisk the eggs in a medium bowl until broken up. Season with a pinch of salt and pepper. Add the remaining 3 tsp. of olive oil to the pan and set it over medium-low heat. Pour in the eggs. Cook and stir until they are softly scrambled, approx. 5 min.

Divide the eggs between the warm tortillas. Top with chorizo, potatoes, cheese, cilantro and salsa.

Fold the sides over the filling and roll them up into burritos.

Serve warm.

Enjoy

Chipotle Chicken Burritos

Prep: 15 min. Cook: 15 min. Ready in: 30 min. Servings: 4

Ingredients:

1 tbsp. vegetable oil

¾ cup pico de gallo or fresh salsa

1 chipotle chili in adobo sauce, chopped + 1-2 tbsp. sauce from can

1 (14 oz.) can pinto beans, drained and rinsed

1 ½ cups shredded chicken, skin removed

¼ cup roughly chopped fresh cilantro

Kosher salt

4 tortillas

1 1/3 cups cooked white rice, warmed

1 1/3 cups cheddar cheese

1 1/3 chips shredded romaine lettuce

Guacamole for serving

Cooking Directions:

Start by heating the vegetable oil in a medium pot over medium-high heat. Add ½ cup pico de gallo, the chopped chipotle, and adobo sauce to taste. Cook until the mixture starts to sizzle, approx. 2 min.

Add the beans and ¾ cup water, bring to a low boil, then stir in the chicken and cook until the mixture is slightly thickened, approx. 2 min. Stir in the cilantro and season with salt.

Heat the tortillas in the microwave or the oven.

Arrange the tortillas with rice in the center of each tortilla. Top with the cheese, chicken mixture, lettuce and the remaining pico de gallo.

Fold in the sides of each tortillas of roll up into burritos.

Serve warm.

Enjoy

Shredded Mexican Chicken Burritos

Prep: 5 min. Cook: 4 h Ready in: 4 h 5 min. Servings: 6

Ingredients:

2 pounds chicken breasts

1 tbsp. olive oil

½ cup salsa

3-4 tbsp. brown sugar

1 (4 oz.) can mild diced green chilies

1 (14.5 oz.) can diced tomatoes, drained

1 tbsp. chili powder

1 ½ tsp. salt

1 tsp. ground cumin

1 tsp. garlic powder

1 tsp. onion power

½ tsp. smoked paprika

½ tsp. dry oregano

½ tsp. pepper

½ tsp. ground chipotle chili pepper

1 tsp. liquid smoke

6 tortillas

Cooking Directions:

Start by rubbing the chicken breasts with oil and place them in the bottom of the slow cooker. Add all of the remaining ingredients. Cook the chicken on high for 2-4 hours or on low for 6-7 hours or until the chicken is tender enough to shred.

Remove the chicken to a cutting board, and let rest for 5 min. before shredding. Save the liquid. Return the shredded chicken and let cook on low for an additional 20 min. to absorb some the liquid. Drain the excess liquid.

Warm the tortillas in the oven or the microwave.

Assemble the burritos by spreading a few spoonsful of the chicken to each of the tortillas. Top off with condiments of your liking.

Serve warm.

Enjoy

Mojo Chicken Burritos

Prep: 60 min. Cook: 1 h 30 min. Ready in: 2 h 30 min. Servings: 8

Ingredients:
For the Mojo Sauce:
4 garlic cloves
2 serrano chilies, seeds removed
1 large handful fresh cilantro leaves
Juice of 2 limes
 Juice of 1 orange
½ cup extra-virgin olive oil
Kosher salt and freshly ground black pepper
For the Yellow Rice:
2 cups long-grain rice
4 cups water
2 cloves garlic, smashed
1 tsp. turmeric
1 tsp. kosher salt
1 bay leaf
For the Spicy Black Beans
2 cups dried black beans, picked over and rinsed
3 tbsp. extra-virgin olive oil
1 medium onion, chopped
1 jalapeno pepper, chopped
2 cloves garlic, chopped
1 bay leaf
Kosher salt and black pepper
For the Burritos:
8 tortillas
1 (3-4 pound) whole roasted chicken, shredded
2 avocados, chopped
1 cup grated queso blanco or Monterey Jack cheese
Sour cream, for garnish
Cilantro leaves, for garnish

Cooking Directions:

Start by putting the beans in a pot and cover with water by 2 inches. Bring to a boil and cook for 2 min. Remove from heat, cover, and let soak for 1 hour. Drain the beans.

In the same pot heat the olive oil. Add the onion, jalapeno pepper, garlic, and bay leaf and cook until the vegetables begin to soften, approx. 5 min. Add the beans and cover with water by 1 inch. Bring to a boil, reduce heat, cover and simmer for 1 to 1 ½ hours, or until the beans are tender. Remove the bay leaf and discard. Taste the beans and season them with salt and pepper.

Next, for the yellow rice, take a pot and put in the rice, water, garlic, turmeric, salt and bay leaf. Bring the mixture to a boil over medium-high heat. Reduce the heat to a simmer, cover and cook over low heat until the rice has absorbed the water, approx. 15-20 min. Remove from the heat and let sit, covered for 5 min. Discard the garlic and bay leaf and set aside to serve.

For the mojo sauce, put the garlic, chilies, cilantro, lime juice, orange juice and olive oil in a blender and process until smooth. Taste and adjust seasoning with salt and pepper.

Warm the tortillas in the oven or in the microwave. Place some chicken in the center of each tortilla and top with rice and beans, avocado, grated cheese and Mojo Sauce. Fold in the sides of the tortillas and roll up into burritos.

Serve warm with sour cream, garnish with cilantro leaves and a squeeze of lime juice.

Enjoy

Tequila-Orange BBQ Chicken Burritos

Prep: 15 min. Cook: 50 min. Ready in: 1 h 5 min. Servings: 4

Ingredients:
3-4 dried New Mexico chili peppers, stemmed and seeded
2 ½ cups chicken stock
1 cup organic ketchup
¼ cup plus 2 tbsp. cider vinegar
2 tbsp. packed dark brown sugar
2 tbsp. Worcestershire sauce
2 tbsp. dark amber maple syrup
2 shots tequila
4 cloves garlic, finely chopped
3 limes
1 small organic orange
1/3 cup plus 1 tbsp. extra-virgin olive oil
4 slices smoky bacon, chopped
1 red onion, halved; 1 half chopped and the other half whole
1 (28 oz.) can baked beans
¼ cup steak sauce
2 tsp. coarsely ground black pepper
1 small red cabbage, finely shredded
Kosher salt
8 tortillas
12 oz. cheddar cheese

Poached Chicken Breasts
4 whole bone-in, skin-on chicken breasts
1 tbsp. whole black peppercorns
8 cloves garlic, smashed
4 large bay leaves
4 carrots, coarsely chopped
4 stalks celery, coarsely chopped
2 lemons, sliced
2 onions, quartered
Herb bundle of fresh parsley, rosemary and thyme tied with kitchen string

Cooking Directions:

Start by putting the chicken in a large pot. Add the peppercorns, garlic, bay leaves, carrots, celery, lemons, onions and herb bundle and sprinkle with salt. Add enough water to cover the chicken. Bring to a boil, then the heat to low and cook at a simmer for 1 ½ hours. Remove the chicken from the liquid and let cool. Strain the stock. Remove the skin and bones from the chicken and shred the meat using 2 forks. Set aside for later use. Toast the chili peppers in a saucepan over medium-high heat, pressing them flag with a spatula and turning occasionally, approx. 2-3 min. Add the stock and bring to a boil. Reduce the heat to a simmer and cook until the chilies are tender, approx. 15-20 min. Puree the chilies and stock in a food processor, then return the mixture to the pan. Add the ketchup, 2 tbsp. vinegar, brown sugar, Worcestershire sauce, maple syrup, tequila and 2 garlic cloves. Grate enough zest from the limes and orange to make 1 tbsp. each. Add to the pan along with the juice of 1 lime and the orange. Reduce the heat to a low boil and cook for 20 min. Add the chicken and stir to coat with the sauce. Meanwhile, heat 1 tbsp. extra-virgin olive oil in a skillet over medium-high heat. Add the bacon and cook until browned. Add the chopped onions and the remaining 2 garlic cloves and cook until soft, approx. 3-4 min. Stir in the beans and cook until heated through. Stir in the steak sauce and pepper. Combine the juice of the remaining 2 limes and the remaining ¼ cup vinegar in a bowl. Grate the remaining onion half into the bowl and whisk in the remaining 1/3 cup extra-virgin olive oil. Add the cabbage and toss to combine. Season with salt and pepper. Drain the slaw before using.

Warm the tortillas in the oven or microwave. Place some of the chicken in the center of each tortillas. Top with cheddar, beans and slaw Fold in the sides of each tortilla and roll them up into burritos. Serve warm.

Enjoy

Chicken and Bean Burritos

Prep: 30 min. Cook: 5 min. Ready in: 35 min. Servings: 4

Ingredients:

4 tsp. olive oil

1 small onion, diced

2 cloves of garlic, minced

½ tsp. ground cumin

1 (15 oz.) can of low-sodium white beans, rinsed and drained

½ cup low sodium chicken broth

½ tsp. salt

2 cups shredded romaine lettuce

1/3 cup fresh cilantro leaves

2 tsp. fresh lime juice

Ground black pepper

4 tortillas

2 cups shredded cooked chicken, skinless

1 jalapeno, finely diced

½ ripe avocado, thinly sliced

½ cup tomatillo salsa

½ cup low-fat Greek-style yogurt

Cooking Directions:

Start by heating 2 tbsp. of the oil in a medium skillet. Add the onion and cook until translucent, approx. 3 min. Add the garlic and cumin and cook for 30 seconds more. Add the beans, broth and ½ tsp. of salt and cook until warmed through, approx. 2 min. Transfer the bean mixture to the bowl of a food processor and process until smooth. Put the lettuce, cilantro, the remaining 2 tsp. of oi, lime juice, a pinch of salt and a few turns of the pepper in a bowl and toss to coat.

Heat the tortillas in the oven or the microwave.

To assemble the burritos, spread 1/3 cup of the bean puree in the center of each tortilla. Sprinkle with about 2 tsp. jalapeno. Top with ½ cup of shredded chicken, then ½ cup of the lettuce mixture and 2 slices of avocado.

Fold in the sides of the tortillas and roll them up into burritos. Serve warm with salsa and yogurt alongside.

Enjoy

Turkey Chili Burritos

Prep: 15 min. Cook: 30 min. Ready in: 45 min. Servings: 6

Ingredients:

1 pound ground turkey

1 tbsp. crushed garlic

1 tbsp. extra-virgin olive oil

1 cup red bell peppers, drained and chopped

1 medium red onion, peeled and diced

2 cups marinara

½ jar jalapeno peppers with chipotle

½ cup fresh cilantro, chopped

1 ½ tbsp. stuffed olives, chopped

1 tsp. chili powder

1 tsp. ground cumin

½ tsp. black pepper

6 tortillas

1 cup shredded jack cheese

4 cups shredded iceberg lettuce

Sour cream, to serve

Salt to taste

Cooking Directions:

Start by taking a large skillet and place it over medium-high heat. Stir in the turkey, garlic, olive oil, bell pepper and onion.

Break the turkey apart until the juices evaporate and the turkey meat is lightly browned, approx. 15 min.

Add the chili powder, ground cumin and pepper. Stir and cook for 2 min. Then add the marinara sauce, jalapenos, cilantro and olives. Stir often, until the flavours are blended, approx. 10 min.

Meanwhile warm the tortillas in the oven or microwave.

To assemble the burritos, spoon the turkey mixture down the center of each tortilla. Top equally with hot sauce, cheese, lettuce and sour cream. Fold in the sides of the tortillas and roll up into a burrito. Serve warm.

Enjoy

Turkey Burritos with Salsa and Cilantro

Prep: 20 min. Cook: 20 min. Ready in: 40 min. Servings: 6

Ingredients:

3 tbsp. olive oil

2 red onions, sliced

2 bell peppers, seeded, sliced

4 cups leftover cooked turkey meat, diced

¾ cup purchased fresh fire-roasted salsa

1 tbsp. ground cumin

1 (8 oz.) package grated 4-cheese blend

¾ cup chopped fresh cilantro

6 tortillas

Cooking Directions:

Start by heating the oil in a skillet over medium-high heat. Add the onions and bell peppers. Sauté until tender and golden, approx. 15 min. Add the turkey, salsa and cumin. Stir until heated through, approx. 5 min. Stir in the cheese and cilantro. Season with salt and pepper.

Remove from heat and cover to keep warm.

Heat the tortillas in the oven or in the microwave.

Take the tortillas and spoon 1 cup of warm turkey mixture along the center of each tortilla.

Fold the sides of the tortillas over the filling and then roll them up into burritos.

Serve warm.

Enjoy

Teriyaki Turkey Burritos

Prep: 20 min. Cook: 20 min. Ready in: 40 min. Servings: 6

Ingredients:

1 pound

½ cup onion, chopped

4 garlic cloves, minced

1 package (16 oz.) broccoli coleslaw mix

1 tbsp. canola oil

1/3 cup teriyaki sauce

½ tsp. Chinese five-spice powder

¼ tsp. garlic powder

¼ tsp. pepper

1 ½ cups (6 oz.) shredded Mexican cheese blend

6 tortillas

Cooking Directions:

Start by taking a skillet and placing it over medium heat. Cook the turkey, onion and garlic until the turkey is no longer pink, drain the skillet and pour the meat into a bowl and set aside.

In the same skillet, stir-fry broccoli in oil for 2 min. Add the teriyaki sauce, five-spice powder, garlic powder and pepper. Cook and stir for 1 min. Stir in cheese and turkey mixture, heat through.

Spoon about ½ cup filling off center on each tortilla. Fold the sides of each tortilla over the filling and roll up into burritos.

Serve warm.

Enjoy

Turkey and Black Bean Burritos

Prep: 5 min. Cook: 15 min. Ready in: 20 min. Servings: 6

Ingredients:

1 pound ground turkey

1 tsp. oil

1 (15 oz.) can black refried beans

Salt and pepper to taste

Juice of ½ lime

6 tortillas

2 cups cooked rice

1 ½ - 2 cups shredded Mexican blend cheese

Shredded lettuce, for garnish

Chopped tomato, for garnish

Cilantro leaves, for garnish

Sour cream, for garnish

Salsa, for garnish

Cooking Directions:

Start by taking a large skillet and heat the oil over medium heat. Add ground turkey and cook until browned, approx. 5 min. Stir in 1 can of black refried beans and continue to cook until liquid is reduced, approx. 3-5 min. Squeeze in juice from half a lime.

Assemble the burritos by taking each tortilla and spread a line of rice in the center. Top with turkey, bean mixture, cheese, lettuce, tomato, salsa and sour cream.

Fold in the sides of each tortilla and roll them u into burritos.

Serve warm.

Enjoy

Cajun Rice and BBQ Turkey Burritos

Prep: 5 min. Cook: 20 min. Ready In: 25 min. Servings: 4

Ingredients:

½ pound leftover cooked turkey

1 red pepper, deseeded

2 sticks of celery, chopped

1 fresh red chili, sliced

6 spring onions, sliced

2 cloves of garlic, sliced

1 bunch of coriander, leaves picked, stalks sliced

Olive oil

Sea salt

Ground black pepper

½ pound of precooked wholegrain rice

1 lemon, juice and zest

3 tbsp. BBQ sauce

4 tortillas

1 oz. feta cheese

Low-fat natural yoghurt, to serve

Cholula hot chili sauce, to serve

Cooking Directions:

Start by taking a frying and placing it over high heat with a drizzle of olive oil. Add the red pepper, celery, chili, spring onions, garlic, coriander and season with salt and pepper. Fry for approx. 5 min, or until soft, stirring regularly. Add the rice, lemon zest and juice and cook for a further 5 min, or until golden and warmed through.

Meanwhile, toss the turkey in the barbecue sauce, then add to a frying pan over medium-high heat and cook for approx. 5-10 min., or until crispy and slightly caramelised.

Warm the tortillas in the oven or microwave.

Divide equal amount of the Cajun rice and turkey on each of the tortillas. Top with the coriander leaves and crumble feta on top.

Fold in the sides of each tortilla and roll them up into burritos.

Serve warm.

Enjoy

Printed in Great Britain
by Amazon